HAIKU MOMENTS

Haiku by

Sue Neufarth Howard

ISBN: 978-1-312-33277-5

ACKNOWLEDGMENTS

Published in

(1) Unitedhaikuandtankasociety.com/
    cattails, January, 2014
(2) accents-publishing.com for
    Lexington Poetry Day 2014,
    2013
(3) High Coupe online journal,
    kindofahurricanepress.com
(4) Storm Cycle – 2013 Best Of
    Anthology,
    kindofahurricanepress.com

These poems are for Jennifer,
Kalinda, and Karlie, with special thanks
to poets from the Greater Cincinnati
Writers League and Linton St.
Writers.

spent blossoms

floating

white petal snow

prolonged song;

wind chimes

pushy breeze

April wears

pink and white flowered bonnets,

yellow-freckled lawns

stilled robin on the road;

what happens to babies

in the nest?

April sun

two turtles

on the pond log

March tease

tempt to sprout

then freeze

spring

on the trees overnight

petals like popcorn

monkey-faced pansies

bobble-headed by the wind

nod good afternoon (3)

young tree leaves

breeze tickled

giggle   laugh   wiggle

birth announcement
three tiny goslings
mom herds around the pond

in the wind
grey-purple leaf shadows
dancing

day's-end taps
owl calls
in the fading light

evening stroll;
on the sidewalk
broken robin's egg

the pond turtle
head butts her newborn
back under the bridge

white petals, night wind;
seeds of stars sprinkled in
moonlit silver gardens   (3)

in the morning hush

of quiet forest green

what I see sees me

Scallops;
squirrel leaps across
the lawn   (1)

mamma walks the sky
at night sowing moonbeams
seeds of poems   (4)

steps away

twelve geese don't see me

seated pond side

rain drops

tadpoles on panes

race to puddle

sun sparkles
on pond ripples - glittering,
dancing like stars on speed

first morning light;
moon's tears on the grass
glisten

making figure eights,
soar-searching
hungry hawks

in shade of
breeze-tossed summer trees
dark lace dancing   (2)

half buried

in the muddy bog

meditative eye

fluttering wings

hovering mystically

the Humming Bird sips   (2)

its cover blown

the turtle beats a hasty retreat

from the Dachshund's din (2)

a side-walked earthworm –
after the soaker rain
it squiggles in s curves

curlicue twig
what its tree will do
to find the sun

on the asphalt

black and amber, coiled and still

beaded leather choker (2)

robin, beak full streaks

across open sky; what radar

tracks which tree is home (3)

pink dusk

half moon

night light bright

young leaves quiver

like fountain pond ripples

gusting wind tickles

white butterflies
summer fairies in the garden
like dancing lace

art to be found;
on the bone-dry sidewalk
the Rorschach art of drizzle (2)

winged one

somewhere in flight

one feather lighter

fall-cool August
evoking father's fall leaf
burning ritual

(Senryu) (1)

August dusk
last hummingbird
at the feeder

among dropped red/gold leaves
dry curling into brown
one pale pink feather

rust and mustard mums
poke through mounded leaves
plunk!   walnut smack

harvest time
trees still green drop
brown confetti

cloudless azure sky
rice paper afternoon moon
red leaves lay dying

like flying snowflakes

caramel-colored floaters

breakdance in the wind

bare tree fingers

tickle the belly of sky;

it laughs so hard it cries

with a heavy hand
big brush and thick paint
this forest is white washed

branches in winter sun
crystal cover glistens;
in the wind…clink

forest branches
bald – a playground
for gymnastic squirrels   (3)

white flakes
dancing wildly in the wind;
teaser snow

thimble full of sun warmth

February's Fools Gold

bare branches

brush   clack   tangle;

brusque wind

wild, wet, naked joy;

oh to be five once again

dancing in the rain (2)

mellow outside

still a girl on the inside

his glance lingering

(Senryu) (1)

one ladies black spike heel

in a Walmart parking lot

abandoned

ladies at lunch

one sits Indian style

in the restaurant booth

in the studio

creeps a wintered-over stink bug;

death by paint brush

blasting radio rap;

at the pump, dude refuels

groovin' to the beat

(Senryu)

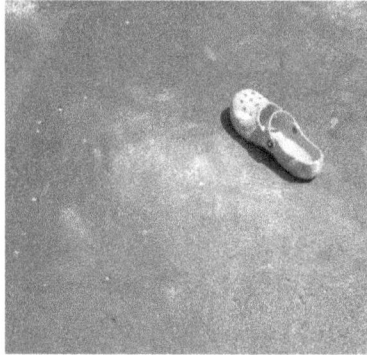

on the hot pavement

someone goes

with one foot bare

sign on the vet mobile
happy tails to you

in the doctor's waiting room
seniors peruse magazines
young bloods check messages
(2)

at the

teller window

the banker takes her cash;

no break in depositor's cell

phone call

(Tanka) (2)

the cat's tummy time

on my lap; I doze to a

purr-fect lullaby (3)

my brain teaser

Alzheimer's keep-away play

write a poem a day (2)

www.ingramcontent.com/pod-product-compliance
Lightning Source LLC
Chambersburg PA
CBHW022349040426
42449CB00006B/800